AF228281

# Wild About Wheels

# MILITARY Vehicles

by Melissa Abramovitz

Consulting Editor: Gail Saunders-Smith, PhD

Consultant: Christopher J. Semancik, MEd
Curriculum Writer, U.S. Army Curator, Educator

CAPSTONE PRESS
a capstone imprint

Pebble Plus is published by Capstone Press,
1710 Roe Crest Drive, North Mankato, Minnesota 56003
www.capstonepub.com



**Library of Congress Cataloging-in-Publication Data**
Abramovitz, Melissa, 1954– author.
Military vehicles / by Melissa Abramovitz.
        pages cm. — (Pebble plus. Wild about wheels)
Summary: "Simple text and full-color photographs describe eight differerent vehicles used by military personnel"— Provided by publisher.
  Audience: Ages 4–8.
  Audience: K to grade 3.
  Includes bibliographical references and index.
  ISBN 978-1-4914-2116-1 (library binding) — ISBN 978-1-4914-2357-8 (ebook PDF)
  1. Vehicles, Military—Juvenile literature. 2.  Armored vehicles, Military—Juvenile literature. I. Title.
  UG446.5.A264 2015
  623.7'4—dc23                                         2014032596

**Editorial Credits**
Nikki Bruno Clapper, editor; Janet Kusmierski, designer; Tracy Cummins, media researcher; Laura Manthe, production specialist

**Photo Credits**
DIVIDS: Master Sgt. Paul Tuttle, 9, Petty Officer 3rd Class Kathleen Gorby, 21, Staff Sgt. Jeremy Wilson, 11, U.S. Marine Corps/Cpl. Christopher J. Moore, 7; Shutterstock: A Periam Photography, 15, aarrows, Design Element, Eugene Berman, 13; Thinkstock: Stocktrek Images, 5, Stocktrek Images, 17; U.S. Army: photo by Gertrud Zach, Cover; U.S. Navy: photo by General Dynamics Electric Boat, 19.

## Note to Parents and Teachers

The Wild About Wheels set supports national curriculum standards for science related to engineering design, forces and interactions, and structure and properties of matter. This book describes and illustrates military vehicles. The images support early readers in understanding the text. The repetition of words and phrases helps early readers learn new words. This book also introduces early readers to subject-specific vocabulary words, which are defined in the Glossary section. Early readers may need assistance to read some words and to use the Table of Contents, Glossary, Read More, Internet Sites, Critical Thinking Using the Common Core, and Index sections of the book.

Printed in the United States of America.
022017         010302R

# Table of Contents

# Military Vehicles

Military vehicles travel on land, at sea, and in the air. They attack enemies, deliver soldiers and supplies, and rescue injured people.

# Land Power

Battle tanks move on tracks.

The M1A1 Abrams tank weighs

almost 68 tons (62 metric tons).

Armor protects four soldiers

inside the tank.

tracks

Transport vehicles carry
troops and supplies. A heavy
equipment transporter (HET)
carries tanks. It is almost as
long as a basketball court.

# Air Power

Fighter planes and bombers do battle in the sky. The B-2 Spirit stealth bomber flies 9 miles (14 kilometers) high. Its shape hides it from enemies.

Cargo planes carry soldiers and supplies. C-5 Galaxies can carry five helicopters, six trucks, or two M1A1 Abrams tanks.

Helicopters can take off and land anywhere. Seahawk helicopters shoot torpedoes at enemy submarines.

# Sea Power

Aircraft carriers are longer

than three football fields.

They carry fighter planes

and about 6,000 crew members.

Attack submarines patrol underwater. Virginia-class submarines are 400 feet (122 meters) long. They carry 134 sailors.

Mine-hunting ships find and
destroy underwater mines.
Avenger-class minehunters
hold 84 sailors. The U.S.
Navy has 14 of these ships.

# Glossary

**armor**—a protective covering made of metal or another hard material

**cargo**—objects carried by a ship, aircraft, or other vehicle

**HET**—a large truck that carries battle tanks; HET stands for heavy equipment transporter

**military**—the armed forces of a state or country

**mine**—an explosive device; water mines float in the water

**patrol**—to protect and watch an area

**stealth bomber**—an aircraft built with special materials and a shape that helps it avoid being found by enemy radar

**supplies**—materials needed to do something

**torpedo**—an underwater missile used to blow up a target

# Read More

**Abramovitz, Melissa.** *Military Airplanes.* Military Machines. Mankato, Minn.: Capstone Press, 2012.

**Peppas, Lynn.** *Powerful Armored Vehicles.* Vehicles on the Move. New York: Crabtree Pub., 2012.

**Von Finn, Denny.** *B-2 Stealth Bombers.* Epic: Military Vehicles. Minneapolis: Bellwether Media, 2013.

# Internet Sites

FactHound offers a safe, fun way to find Internet sites related to this book. All of the sites on FactHound have been researched by our staff.

Here's all you do:

Visit *www.facthound.com*

Type in this code: 9781491421161

# Critical Thinking Using the Common Core

1. How do tanks protect the soldiers who ride in them? (Key Ideas and Details)

2. What is a mine? How do soldiers get rid of water mines? (Craft and Structure)

# Index



Word Count: 179
Grade: 1
Early-Intervention Level: 21